Dr. Bob's Instant RING JUGGLING Book

Featuring more than 50 original ways to throw, catch, spin, flip, bounce, toss and play with rings!

by Bob Woodburn, Ed. D.
Illustrated by Zoltan Csonti

Acknowledgments and Thanks!

For friendship and meritorious service way above and beyond the call of duty:

Zoltan Csonti - illustrations;
Linda Gustafson - cover layout/design;
Keifer Waldron - book layout/design;
Lionel Koffler; Ray Wismer; Diana Robertson; Stuart Fraser; Bill Oliver.

For inspiration and loving support- my touchstones:
Brenda, Karma, Jenna, Adrienne, Clay, John, Jane and all the other wonderful family and friends I am blessed with (and Tia!).

For their encouragement, time and enormous help, all the following:

Alan Amaral; Jesse Dryden; Tom Slater & his drama class at Ross; Adies friends; Jim Lewis & the art class at Wilfrid Laurier; Robyn Ford; Brian & Don Wilson, Suzie Howell; Krista & Carol Hermann, Keith Petitt- The Simply Wonderful Wonders; Nancy Case; Ron Belanger; Ron Hearnden & The Webcom Crew; John MacDonnel; Graham Fletcher; Cheryl Tien; Graham & D'Arcy Davis; the Robertson Pick Gang; Damien Gryski; John McIntyre; Mark Goldberg, Sue Buchanan & Amy; The Pattisons- Ian, Lynn, Kaitlin, Emily, Sam & Diva; The Bresnahans-Kit, Pam, Andrew & Sara; Kim Rowland; Wendy Jackson; The Toronto Juggling Club; Julie Cosgrave; Ken Hood & The Bookshelf Folks; Ken Ryall- Tru Moulded; Owen Scott; Kim Denstedt.

And all the other unsuspecting passersby who wandered innocently into my line of sight and helped make this project stronger and more like play than work!

ISBN 0-9694324-1-0

Distribution by: Firefly Books Ltd.
3680 Victoria Park Avenue,
Willowdale, Ontario, Canada
M2H 3K1

Printed and bound in Canada
Dr. Bob's Instant Juggling™ Rings made in Canada

"I can barely find the snooze button on my alarm, but I actually learned to juggle rings with Dr. Bob."

Adrienne Kistner (age 17)

	Page
Acknowledgments	2
Introducing Dr. Bob	4
Dr. Bob's Juggling Tricks	13
Bounces	14
Spins	22
Flips	28
Smorgasbord Safari	33
UFR's (Unidentified Flying Rings)	43
Routines	50
Partners, Passing and "Numbers"	51
Products, Workshops and Website Info	63

Introducing Dr. Bob.....

I seem to attract the most unusual students. They say I have a knack for making it easy! So my juggling proteges wanted to be here to welcome you to this wonderful activity-you'll love it! It will make you famous just like it did for them!

For those of you who are total beginners, juggling "challenged" or even, horror of horrors, juggling "deprived", RELAX. *You'll learn this quickly and easily.*

> "It's as easy as catching a cold."   *Graham Fletcher* (age 34)

And for those who can juggle for at least a few seconds, get ready to add lots of **spins, flips, bounces, passes, and numbers** to your juggling fun.

> "I can already juggle, but I was amazed at all the fun variations I got into. You blew my seasoned juggling socks right off, Dr. Bob".
> *Stuart Fraser* (age 27)

4

Important Stuff Everyone Needs to Read First!

Tip I — Have Fun and Be Safe

Juggling rings is safe and great fun! However, they are hard objects! So be smart, use your head (not literally) and pick your juggling places and tricks carefully.

Tip II — Begin With the 4 Easy Steps

Even if you already juggle, look at the beginning instructions / p. 6. There are some very helpful hints on ring "technique" for everyone.

Tip III — Dr. Bob's Tricky Ratings

A number of tricks are rated with Dr. Bob's special icons so you can go right to them if you want.

 So **Easy** it's shameful

 So **Hard** it's laughable

Tip IV — The Basic Start Position

This basic start position is where the fun begins. It's how you hold the three rings to begin almost all the tricks.

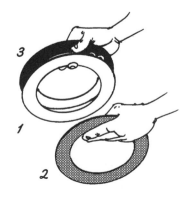

Ring Juggling In Four
Easy Steps

Once your friends have moved all the crystal and their special antiques, get ready, and have a blast.

Step 1

The Grip

♦ Pick up one ring in the hand you usually favor, the one you write or throw with. This is your **Start Hand**, the hand you will **always** begin a trick with. Hold the ring lightly, as shown, with gentle but firm pressure - no death grips yet!

The Stance

♦ Find a place with good light and high ceilings. Stand easy, feet apart, knees slightly flexed, elbows bent at your sides.

The Throw

♦ Toss the first ring lightly from one hand to the other, PAUSE - **then toss it back** (in an arc about two feet above your head and one foot in front of you) with a slight **backspin** to steady it. Do this a number of times. Don't rush - take your time.

♦ Follow through and up with your hand and fingers as you throw.

♦ As the ring comes back down, reach up to catch.

♦ Counting **Out Loud** really helps as you first learn. Say "**one**" out loud *as you* **let the ring go** (not after you release it). Do ten throws back and forth **R ➜ L** and back **L ➜ R**. Each time, follow the ring's arc with your eyes all the way.

Step 2

Place one ring in each hand. Note which hand you naturally favor and start with that hand. This will always be your **Start Hand** used to begin every trick from now on.

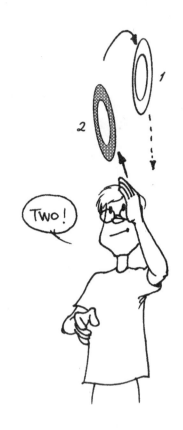

♦ TIMING IS EVERYTHING! With one ring in each hand, Toss the first ring up and say "**ONE**". As soon as you finish saying "**ONE**" (it's at it's peak) toss the second ring up across **and under** the first ring and say "**TWO**". Catch each ring in turn and stop. Repeat this a number of times. Pretend that you are hitting two magic "spots" and are working in a shoulder-width frame.

♦ Note that you **swing** your hand towards the inside and send the second ring straight up the center line of your body. This is a natural motion. Even though each ring starts up the center line of your body, it will move naturally towards a spot above your opposite shoulder. The gap between the rings at their peak should be about shoulder width.

♦ **Remember**... Don't pass the second ring across from one hand to the other. **Each ring must go up in an arc and over!**

♦ If you do find yourself passing the rings straight across rather than up and over, try starting with your other hand first (the non-start hand) to break that nasty habit immediately. After trying this a few times you will see which hand is easiest to begin with.

♦ Avoid experiencing ring "smash" from throwing both rings at the same time. Pay attention to the **pause** between the release of ring 1 and ring 2. You know you're *not* allowing for it, when both rings come down at the same time.

♦ Take the **Basic Start Position**, ie. holding two rings in your **Start Hand** and one in the other hand.

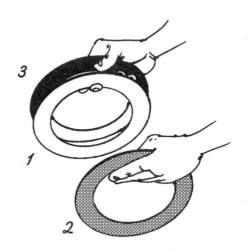

♦ Do exactly the same as you did in step two.

♦ Practice tossing the first two rings **(1 & 2)** back and forth as before, counting "1...2". Ring three (the one in the heel of your hand) **is not used yet**, just held there.

♦ **Stop**! after each complete tossing of the two rings as in step two. Now you've set the stage for the three ring circus!

Step 3 Continued- The 3 Ring Circus!

♦ Now stretch your counting to **1...2...3...** and **anticipate** tossing the third ring up. *As soon as* you finish saying "**TWO**", say "**THREE**" and move your hand **as if** you are going to send it - but don't let it go yet! Try this fake move twice.

♦ Now try all of the rings for the first time. Throw all rings **1...2...3...** and don't try to catch any of them - let them hit the floor and listen to the rhythm, it should be even i.e. **1 and 2 and 3** (like a music count). Do this step twice.

♦ **Remember:** Every time you say a number, you release a ring **immediately**, as you say it.

♦ Now try this again, send **1...2...3...** and catch as many as you can. You may grab one or none - don't worry, keep trying.

♦ Folks usually hang on to the third ring too long. So send the third ring **sooner** by counting **1... 2.3** (like doing the polka) tossing the third ring a little quicker, ie. **right after** you finish saying "**TWO**" and have tossed the second one.

Continuous Juggling - The Cascade Pattern

o the same as Step 3, then begin to **anticipate** making the fourth toss the same as you did ith the third. Count **1...2...3...4...** and note which hand the fourth toss is coming from, but on't send it up yet. Do this twice.

♦ The method for the fourth toss is exactly the same as you did for ring 3 (ie. as soon as you're finished saying "THREE"-out loud, that's the time to let the fourth one go and say "FOUR"). Do it and then **Stop** after you've done four tosses. Remember to say the numbers out loud and send the fourth one **as soon** as you say "THREE". Don't worry if you don't catch the fourth one...or any of them for that matter. You will!

♦ After four tosses and catches you'll have two rings **back in the same hand you started with**. Do this step a number of times. Once you can complete these four consecutive tosses and catches, **Go For Continuous Juggling**.

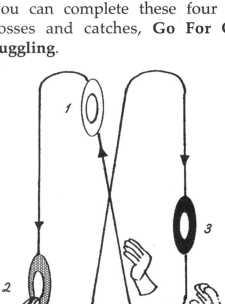

♦ Now, **don't stop counting** or throwing at four. Just keep going no matter what. First you may only get to five or six, then drop back to three, then go up to eight, then back to five etc., until EUREKA! you've got it - CONTINUOUS JUGGLING! It's called the "CASCADE" PATTERN and it looks like a figure 8 on it's side. **It's the key connecting pattern that most tricks start from and return to.**

Check out **Dr Bob's Tricky Tips-**They Help! (Next page and throughout the book).

ice Going! Your life (a.k.a. the 3-ring circus) will never be the same. You'll be invited every-here I bet, even to the White House...or at least the green one down the street!

s you move deeper into this mysterious and wonderful world of flying ring objects, you'll see e true purpose of life. It's an outrageous game and we should play it that way, with great usto! Have fun!

Dr. Bob's Tricky Tips

♦ It may take a little longer than you thought, but stick with it! Your pace of learning is perfect and **you can do this!**

♦ **Take breaks!** Otherwise, you might start to feel wingy (or ringy!).

♦ Get a close family friend (or the dog) to watch a help you figure out what's going on.

♦ **Relax...   Slow Down**! Your rings love R & B (F & Bounce) and wind up in the most unus places. So try it over your bed.

♦ **Count out loud 1...2...3... and watch**

♦ **Watch the flight path** of the rings closely. Glue your eyes to the first one until it's at its peak (when you finish saying "**two**"), then switch and "eye in" the second and third.

♦ If you're reaching, it's OK. Everyone does it (usually on ring 2 or 3). Try **overcompensating** and make those rings curl back and hit the invisible magic spots a little closer to you. Or try it a foot or so away from a sturdy dent-proof wall - that will give you the same result.

♦ Carry your rings with you **everywhere,** and practice in short bursts.

Dr. Bob's Ring Juggling Tricks

These great tricks will put a brand new bounce, spin, flip, toss and pass on your juggling fun. Have a blast and put your own unique signature on them.

Bounces

Bounces are fun and inventive. We start with a few easier ones, but don't let that get in the way of your unusual sense of adventure. Dive in wherever you want and play for a while.

And remember our motto: Have fun and be safe!

The Basic Bounce

♦ Toss one ring up about 2-3 feet, keeping the ring vertical with a slight backspin on it. Let it drop to the floor and bounce straight back up into your hand. It bounces great off most hard surfaces (wood, concrete, tile, asphalt) and also firm carpets. *But not* SHAG *carpet* (especially orange).

♦ Now you can begin by throwing the first ring out and up, let it bounce and then go right into your continuous cascade pattern (p. 11) off the bounce.

Or, with your cascade already going, throw one ring a little bit higher (see "Halos on High" p. 34), hold onto the other two (one in each hand), let the one ring bounce, and then carry right on with your cascade again.

It's routine... but never boring!
Congrats! This is your first shot at a juggling "routine" where you string a few tricks together linked by your cascade. Now you can run away and join the circus (but maybe don't quit your day job yet). See other routine suggestions on page 50.

Knee Bumps

♦ Start by tossing a **single** ring straight up and a bit lower th[an] usual (head height). As the ring comes down bump it back fr[om] a spot just back of your knee. Do this a number of times to f[ind] the right spot and height for you.

♦ Timing is the key. Keep yo[ur] **eye on the ring** all the w[ay] down and back up to catc[h] in the same hand you sen[t] from. Your knee may smar[t a] little as you first learn, but i[t's a] small price to pay for your a[rt.] Just keep remembering h[ow] famous you'll soon be (like [my] other students) and know th[at] in some primitive juggling c[ul-] tures tiny little discreet brui[ses] are a symbol of status.

♦ Then, once you get used to the bump, pick up three rings and begin your normal cascade juggling. Whenever you feel ready, bounce one of the rings off your knee, catch it, continue juggling, bumping it again, etc.

...he Double Grab Bounce Start

- Hold **all three rings** in your usual **Start Hand**

- Throw all three rings up tight together, and a little higher than usual.

- Wait...while they split and open up from each other on the way up.

- **As they peak,** grab the outside two quickly.

GRAB   GRAB

- **Wait...** again while the middle one bounces up off the floor, then incorporate it right into the start of your cascade pattern. (p. 11).

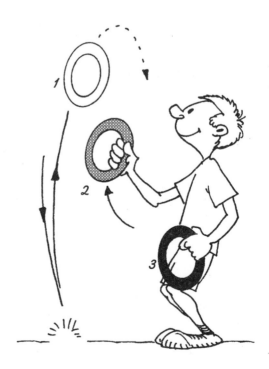

17

Off the Wall

♦ Try bouncing the ring off the floor, onto the wall and then back to you.* Pick your floor and wall carefully so you don't damage either one (or yourself!).

♦ Again, as you flick/snap your wrist down, keep the ring vertical and **follow through** towards the wall, so that there's a forward spin on the ring. It will then bounce quite "true" back to you.

♦ The ring hits the floor 2/3 of the way to the wall.

A Tricky Cascade Version

♦ Hold one ring in your **Start Hand**, one in your other hand, and one tucked up under your arm.

♦ Throw **ring 1** from your **Start Hand** tow the wall. **As soon as** you let it go immediat grab **ring 2** with your **Start Hand** (you r have one ring in each hand).

♦ As the first ring rebounds back off the wall, start your cascade and incorporate it right into the pattern.

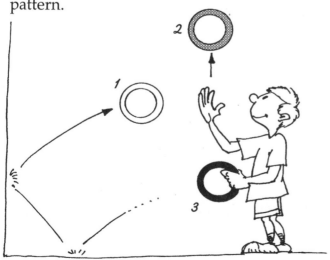

Dr. BoB's
TRICKY
Rx TIP

* If your rings get nicked fr bouncing, take some medi sandpaper and quickly smo them out again.

18

The Old School Yard "Wall Games"

A few fun and off-the-wall versions of traditional school yard games

HORSE

There is **one ring** for the group to use. The person with the ring bounces it off the wall and calls someone's name. The person called has to catch it, **before** it hits the ground (or they get a letter ie. 'H'). Then they immediately throw it back calling someone else's name. When you get all five letters, eg: <u>H O R S E</u> you're outta there.

Adaptation 1: You could adapt this so you get to take a **letter off** if you catch it in a **tricky way** eg: down on your arm or on your foot before throwing it back.

Adaptation 2: Use **two rings**. Two separate people throw them at the same time and each call a person's name. Then continue the same as before.

Adaptation 3: Played the same way as above (calling names out) except now people get **points** for the **type** of catch they make eg: 1-one bounce; 2-in air; 3-on your foot or behind the back etc. The first person to get 21 points is the winner.

Bounce Your Partner

Part One

♦ Start with just **one ring,** between you and stand approximately 15 feet apart. Send it over to your partner, bouncing it off the floor. **Pick a spot to hit about 1/3** of the way towards them. Watch the spot, and use an **easy** wrist snap and follow through.

♦ They catch it and then bounce the same ring back to you. Try this a few times.

Keep the speed down initially or be prepared to replace your partner because they'll be outta there! Remember that dental floss won't work to remove rings: so be alert, pay attention, and **throw easy**.

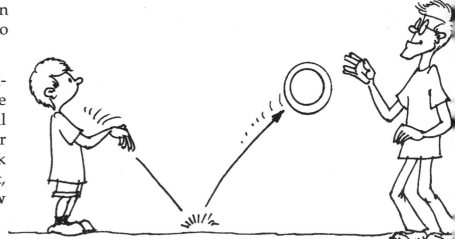

Part Two

♦ Now send **one ring each, at the same time**. Use Dr. Bob's special cue system and **count** i.e. **ready** *and* **go**- both sending your ring on **"go"**. For accuracy, follow through and **watch** the **spot** until your ring hits it - **Then** look up and catch!

A fun adaptation is to see how far you can move back from each other and still do this. It's really fun in the wind!

Later, you can actually work up a whole passing routine off the floor instead of up in the air (see Partnering/Passing p. 52).

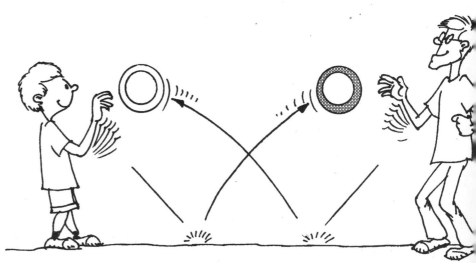

he Big Bracelet Triple

or You

Start by practicing by yourself. Keeping the rings **tight together**, toss the three rings up with a slight backspin. As they bounce back up and peak, drive your hand through all three rings. Then let them slide down into your hand and get ready to start your cascade.

or Your Partner

As before, toss all three rings together and have **your partner** catch **your three rings** driving their arm through all three at once. Make sure the three rings stay close together as they bounce.

For Both of You at Once (the pairs event)

♦ Stand four feet apart facing each other. As you both say *"Ready **and** go!"*, each person throws their three rings up at the same time. Then they drive their hand through your rings and you through theirs (with loud shouts of *"Right-On"* to each other!) Followed by high "3s" with the rings.

SPINS

Spins are kinda goofy, pretty easy and have the potential to add real flavor to your juggling stew. Happy cookin!

Dr. Bob

ut of The Frying Pan... (a sizzling trick)

♦ Hold **ring 1** in your **Start Hand.** Hold **ring 2** flat and steady like a frying pan with your other hand and hold back **ring 3** under this same arm.

Toss **ring 1** straight up giving it a **vigorous backspin snap**. As you catch it - let **ring 2** "give" a bit, so **ring 1** will land smoothly, stay vertical and spin easily (it will spin for a surprising amount of time, with a good backspin snap and a soft catch). Try this a number of times.

♦ Then, before the ring loses its spinning momentum, grab **ring 3** from under your arm with your **Start Hand** and get ready to exchange it with spinning **ring 1** after you flip it up. Then just carry on into your cascade.

D NOW TRY THIS...

Once you get this, keep increasing the **height** of the spin ring as you first send it up. You may have to bend at the knees now in order to "give" enough with the "frying pan" ring.

23

Boomerangs:

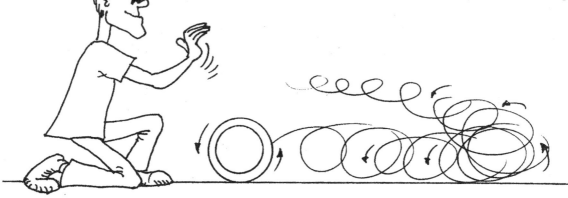

- Holding the one ring you are going to spin with your **Start Hand** and kneeling on the floor, flick the ring **up** about 12"/30cm and **out** about 3'/1m in front of you. Keep it vertical, snapping the wrist down hard as you let it go to give it a very fast backspin. As it hits the floor, it will first bounce a little as it goes out, then spin in place, and finally roll back towards you on its edge.

NOW TRY THIS...

- You can also use this move to start your routine. From a bent-knee bowling type position, backspin one ring out in front of you about three feet, then stand up, and as it rolls back towards you, put your foot through and catch it. Now you're ready to flip it up and start into your routine (see **Flips** p. 29).

AND THIS....

- For a real "kicker"... try backspinning all three **at once** then, as they return, catch one with each hand and hook the third ring on your foot...pause...then flip it up and go right into your cascade pattern.

Dr. BoB's
TRICKY
Rx TIP

Remember to squeeze all three rings tight together (and keep them low to the floor) as you toss and snap down hard.

◆ Start with **one ring** first on the pointer finger on your **Start Hand**. Your arm and **Start Hand** are in their usual start position. Move your pointer finger in small circles to start the ring spinning. Watch the ring seem to change shape and dimension as you speed it up and slow it down. Then slowly bring your arm upright letting the ring heli-spin. Be careful not to let it fly off and bonk your nose.

W TRY THIS...

◆ Do it with the other hand next. Then try it with **both hands** simultaneously. With one ring on the pointer (index) finger of each hand, start the rings spinning on both fingers at the same time. Then bring both arms upright and go for lift-off. It is easiest to start spinning inwards, towards the center line of your body.

◆ Then practice spinning them at the same time outwards (away from the center line). Also try putting two on one finger, and one on the other.

Edge Spins (a.k.a. living on the edge)

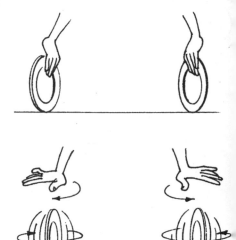

♦ This is done the same as taking a quarter and "snap" spinning it on its edge like a top. The easiest way to do this is to have the ring resting **on the floor** as you spin it. Later you can start its spin **one inch** off the floor for greater snap-speed at startup. Try it with one ring in your **Start Hand** first.

♦ Then do it with both hands **at once** so when you get both rings spinning together, you quickly introduce the third ring into the middle.

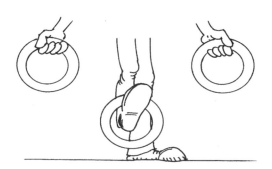

♦ After you set all three spinning and as they start to lose their spin, grab each of the outside o (one per hand) and catch the middle one on your foot (as you stand up).

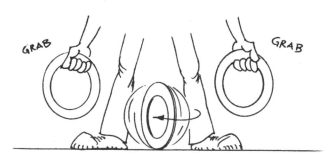

♦ Then kick-up the ring and start into your cascade routine.

NOW TRY THIS...

♦ For you "spin on the edge, numb crazy" dudes, collect all your rings ring type household or office obj and see how many you can get spinn at once.

26

Shoulder Rolls... for all you "roundball" junkies

♦ Flick the ring up very gently with some **easy** backspin. Then stretch your arm and hand **out and up** so the ring lands softly (vertically on its edge) on the back of your outstretched hand and begins to roll slowly down your arm.

♦ As it rolls down your arm, let it pass over your shoulder and down your back, where you can grab it by reaching around to your mid-back.

NOW TRY THIS...

♦ Once you get this, go for the **double arm roll**. Have both arms out as shown. Let the ring roll down your arm, across the back of your neck, down across the other arm and then grab for it.

FLIPS

Flips can drive your adoring audience (and you too) crazy. But they're fun, just be prepared to seek help.

Dr. Bob

Flips
Flips

The Half

♦ Begin by holding one ring out in front of you. Send it up with a **half flip** so that it lands in your hand again, catching it by the opposite edge. Experiment with different degrees of pressure on the ring between your thumb and fingers. Note that while the toss is in your wrist, **the control is in your thumb.**

The Full

♦ Graduate to a **full flip** so you're now catching on the same edge that you started with. Try that a few times and then go to a one and a half, two, three or as many as you feel wacky enough to try.

vo Ring Double

Again, practice with each hand, separately first, then with both simultaneously. Keep your eye carefully on the ring each time.

The One Flip "Floater"

♦ Hold one ring in your left hand (if you are right-handed) straight out in front of you. Reach up with your other hand stretched straight up in the air as high as you can raise it above your head. **Look up** at the hand that's held up high.

♦ Send the ring (with a good follow through) from your left hand with *one full flip* rotation **firmly and quickly** up the other hand. Remember while the to is in your wrist, the **control** comes fro your thumb pressure and placemen And look up!

♦ The key is to not move the hand tha held high above your head, but rather l the ring **come to it** and then grab the ri at the last instant. This trick looks har but it's not ... it's just cool!

e's Flipped His Lid!

♦ Do one full flip from your **Start Hand** up so you can catch it on your head. Watch the ring closely until the last instant, then "duck" under it and "give" a bit as it lands.

It helps to wear a baseball type cap with the peak turned backwards. The cap helps to catch the ring and also protects your noggin' from nasty "ring knock"!

NOW TRY THIS...

♦ Move on to do this with two or even three flips eventually. This is also a great way to start a routine. Flip it up on your head, pause...., then toss the second ring to start your cascade and **immediately** reach up with your **Start Hand,** pull the ring off your head and introduce it into your cascade. (see p. 11)

The Flat... Flip-Flop

Flats

- From your usual cascade pattern (with the rings vertical) catch and turn them 90° so they are now sent up **flat in front of you**, as you face your fans. Do this for one pass.

- Or... Start your cascade with the rings being flat for one pass - then go back to your vertical pattern.

Flips

- Start your cascade by one round of three flips... then return to vertical cascading until your next trick.

- Or... Cascade vertical, then shift to flips for one pass, then return to vertical.

Dr. Bob's
SMORGASBORD SAFARI

A wide variety of very cool, exotic tricks selected for your ring juggling pleasure from the far reaches of the planet, for the adventurous...

Dr. Bob

Halos on High: Saintly Juggling

(or how to buy extra time to set up your next heavenly trick)

- ♦ Polish up your "halo", borrow two others (or use your rings) and take the **Basic Start** position.

You need heavenly ceilings (at least semi high) or the great outdoors for this trick. (Bank lobbies, supermarkets, old houses, or the Taj Mahal work well)

- ♦ Start by throwing the first halo/ring twice as high as usual to begin your cascade pattern and say **"1"** as you send it.

34

♦ Wait **patiently** for it to come down close to your opposite hand, then at your regular height send the second ring up and over and then the third in your usual cascade pattern (count out loud).

♦ Continuing juggling, (and counting) send **"1"** again up twice as high (it now comes out of your **L** hand -if you started **R**) and continue counting and cascading as before, again sending **"1"** up twice as high. Do this for three or four passes, then stop.

Ring 1- The **DHR** (*Designated High Ring*) is sent from **alternate hands**. However, at **any** time in your cascade pattern when you just wish to do this once, or you want to buy some time for a cool trick (or a pattern "break"), you'll want to send it from your best hand (your **Start Hand**) as that is the one you'll likely favor for your upcoming trick.

Fountain of Rings

♦ Take the **Basic Start** position.

♦ **The Two Ring Fountain**
Start juggling just the two rings in your **Start Hand** for three continuous rounds (1-2, 1-2, 1-2) in a fountain pattern above your hand.

♦ And then introduce the third (single) ring up into the **middle** of the other two, continuing right into your normal three ring **cascade** pattern.

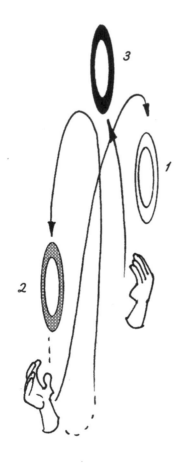

Dr. BOB's TRICKY TIP
Rx

To get consistent height - imagine invisible spot above your head that rings should hit each time.

For a change, try starting the foun with two rings in your other non **S Hand**. Try this with all your tricks ev tually. This leads up to doing **four ri** (O my God!) with two coming from **e** hand simultaneously (see p. 57)

actually there's no smoke, but this is a *HOT* trick!

♦ Cascade juggle in front of a mirror and stand well back, no one needs seven years of bad luck. Don't look at the rings directly, but see them (and yourself) in the mirror.

Talk or sing to yourself, it's a great way to clear the area if you want to be alone!

♦ Then practice this without a mirror by looking *past* the rings at something, or someone else (it really unnerves people when you do this in an elevator or the airport terminal, especially if you grin at them).

♦ **Notice** the rings, especially at the top of their path, but don't watch them too closely.

Down Under... Way to go mate

- Take the **Basic Start** position.

- **To begin**, raise your knee quickly a[nd] toss the **first ring** under that leg. Re[ach] way under with your arm as you t[oss] this ring up and over. Do this th[ree] times with one ring only.

- Then try it on the first throw as y[ou] begin your cascade. Carry on juggl[ing] a few passes and stop.

- Now do your regular cascade juggl[ing] and then, every few tosses, throw [a] ring under your raised right leg a[nd] return to cascade juggling. Repeat t[his] move three times.

NOW TRY THIS...

"Ambidextrous my dear Watson!"

- Try it under the other, farside leg both as a first move, and then from your cascade. It's fun to try all your tricks from both sides...(honest) and you'll probably attract more friends who can then help to free you up when you get stuck in pretzel position #4.

Don't do this one while standing at the edge of the cliffs in Acapulco.

he Hair Raiser (or Ringer)

Version 1:

♦ Unless your friends call you "flat head", you'll need to practice this one with just two rings first. Send **"1"** higher with your right hand. Reach up and place **"2"** on your head (with your left hand) and then quickly reach up to catch **"1"** in your left hand. Tilt your head slightly to let **"2"** slide and fall off slowly.

♦ As **"2"** falls off, toss **"3"** up and over as usual, catch **"2"** and carry on with your cascade again.

rsion 2:

When you get slower and more controlled, keep the ring on your head and then **reach up** with your right hand and actually **take it off**. Then continue your cascade. Eventually you can do this every time (for three passes) and then return to the cascade, before your next trick.

The Back-Up

View from above

♦ Start with only **one ring**. Throw it behind your back with your **Start Hand** so that it curls up and over your shoulder (note that the ring starts out parallel to your back). Look up for it, then catch it with your other hand at chest height.

♦ Pause, then throw it from that non **Start Hand** behind your back again and over your **other** shoulder to catch again in your **Start Hand**.

Now take the **Basic Start** position and begin by sending the front ring (**"1"** of the two held in your **Start Hand**) over behind your back.

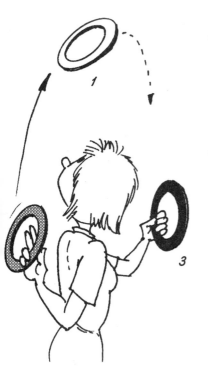

♦ As it appears above your shoulder, throw ring **"2"** over in front of you and begin your cascade juggling. Then stop.

♦ Repeat this step a number of times starting from alternate sides, ie. start with two in your other, non-**Start Hand** and begin the move by throwing the first ring behind your back as before.

♦ Now do this "back-up" move **while** you are doing your cascade juggling pattern.

As you do the cascade, pick a colour of ring you will use (eg. yellow). Then when the yellow ring comes into your **Start Hand** (**"2"** ring in our diagram) **quickly** move it down to reach and throw behind your back. Remember to send the previous ring **"1"** **quite high**, to buy more time.

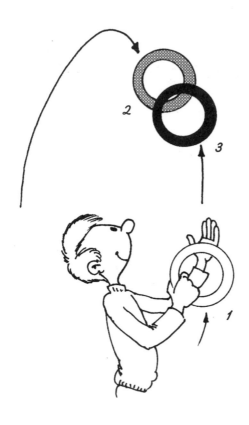

♦ Look for it over your shoulder, and be **patient** - it will likely show up. When it **does**, just keep cascade juggling. However, if it doesn't...**duck**! Then listen -- it **always** tries to hide in really obscure places!

♦ Use the same hand a number of times until you get it. Then try **alternating** with the other hand. Start slowly, using the same steps as before. This is a pretty darn hard trick! but a highly recommended way to test your sanity (and also your housemates!) Go for it!

UFR's (Unidentified Flying Rings)

UFR's and other weird and wonderful tricks
have been expressly flown in for you by

Dr. Bob

Cosmic Rings... Flying with the eagles

♦ This is best done **outside** or in a room with really high ceilin
Start your rings in a cascade at the normal height and th
gradually work your way up to having them go higher a
higher. Then slowly back down again (patience!!).

Your **catching** technique is very important here. Ca
the ring so it first makes contact on the soft part at
base of your thumb and then smoothly let your ha
"give" as you grab and complete the catch.

Bright Fireworks

♦ It looks spectacular to start low, then suddenly **send** the rings up very high
in a burst, like a roman candle and then quickly back down again. This is
great practice for working up to juggling four, five, and six rings (p. 57).

The Flash, Clap and Pivot

♦ Try the **flash move.** Send all three rings up **quicker,
higher and in close succession**, "clap", then catch
and repeat, or go into your controlled cascade.

♦ Then try this. While clapping, quickly **pivot
around** in a circle, re-catch and carry on.

As soon as you catch, re-throw in **rapid succession** 1- 2- 3,
then clap. Or for a real thrill try letting all the rings bounce off
the floor, wait, then catch the outside two as they peak and
quickly return to cascade (see p. 11)

Quoits Up Doc?

The ancient game of Quoits, where you pitched round objects on pins, is our inspiration for this next trick. Here are **three nifty variations** on this theme of pitching your rings onto a target. The target could be a partner's hand, a bowling pin, a tree branch, or even your little brother (just kidding).

Remember: Toss gently! Be safe. Have fun.

Version 1:

Toss one ring onto a stationary object like a stick, a branch or someone's arm held up high.

Version 2:

Toss two rings onto two objects that are close together. Note the two rings overlapping to start and the **sideways** arm/hand motion used, keeping your eye on the targets and using good **follow through** technique.

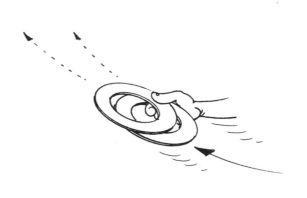

Start with someone holding a stick and/or wearing gloves until the trick is perfected.

45

Version 3:

Use lots of rings: three, four or five plus. An act from a famous circus troupe features one person "spray throwing" **nine** rings at once, and having them land simultaneously onto **three** persons' two arms with the third ring settling cleanly over each of their heads, without anyone having to move. (Go with rings on arms first, our rings are a little small for the over-the-head bit).

We've got the extra rings available for you **(for ordering information see p. 63).** All you need is the bodies to be your trusting "helpers".

46

For those odd occasions when one of your rings develops a mind of its own... and "accidentally" drops to the floor. Be a true showman and act like **it's part of your plan.**

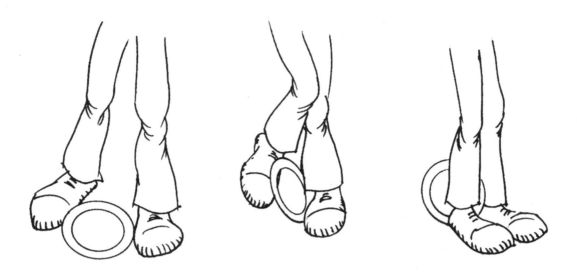

♦ **Big Foot** - After the ring splats on the floor, stop juggling and **ever so casually**, put one foot on each side of the ring, pinch it and stand it up between your feet.

♦ Then, with a smile, **"Kick up your heels!"**, sending it up above your shoulder and then turning quickly towards the ring, catch it, or go smoothly right back into your cascade pattern and say (ever so casually) "Please, hold your applause".

UFR's

These rings make great flying saucers. Just note that they are much harder than the usual flying disc type object and therefore more challenging to catch softly.

 Remember to have a "go with the flow" attitude. Move under the ring as it begins to lose its speed and momentum, and "give" with your hand as you catch it.

A "Rings of Saturn" Start:

♦ Hold the three rings overlapping in your **Start Hand.**

♦ Throw the three rings up on their sides at a (45°) angle with a **slight twist-spin motion** on release, so they do separate from each other. Then catch the outside two as they **peak** (one ring in each hand) and the **middle** ring as it comes down, on your foot.

♦ Then do the **kick-up** and start into your cascade (p. 26).

he Search for the Perfect Ring

reative ring juggling possibilities for home or office

t home...

- **Food Flips:** bagels, donuts, pancakes, pizzas.

- **The Big Round Up:** old hula hoops, bike tires, phonograph records, CDs.

- **Kitchen Art:** cake pans, pot lids, pie plates.

And at the office...

Waste baskets; computer discs; paper rolls; three "ring" binders; toilet seats (only if you're really desperate).

Be prepared, your mom (or your boss) may not like this!

49

And just so it doesn't get too "Routine" around here!

Try one of Dr. Bob's Authentic Three Ring Routine prescriptions. Feel free to adap or change them around, to better suit your "performance".

Face Audience
- Start with a high throw (halo on high)
- Into cascade for ten throws
- Under right leg once (down under)
- Back to cascade five throws
- Fountain of rings for five throws (both hands)
- Five cascade throws and turn

Sideways to audience
- Ten high throws (halo on high)
- Five cascade throws
- Extra high throw (halo) to catch/finish & bow, to great applause!

Basic

Sideways to Audience
- Out of the frying pan start, then cascade for five throws, turning to

Face audience, and go under strong leg three times
- Cascade for five throws
- Flip ring once, flat rings twice
- Cascade five throws
- Ring spin three times
- Cascade for five throws
- Hair raiser two times and turn

Sideways to audience
- Cascade for three throws- then on last cascade throw final ring back up and over head, turn, catch and resume cascade.
- Ring flash, clap and catch all three for finale... and the fans go wild!

Intermediate

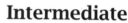

Face Audience
- High double-grab bounce start
- Cascade for five throws
- Under alternate legs three times
- Drop bounce three times
- Reverse cascade for ten throws and turn

Sideways to audience
- Isolate ring behind back twice
- Drop flip toss to foot
- Back to cascade
- High throw with "finish" i.e. send last ring high with backspin, let it bounce, then you pirouette & catch behind your back... and your fame spreads.

Advanced

Partners, Passing and Numbers!

This part will really bond you with your buddies.

Dr. Bob

Partnering, Passing and other 'together' tricks!

There are two variations of this. **Occasionally** taking the rings away each time you are ready; or taking them **every time**, so the rings go back and forth rapidly between partners.

◆ Your partner has the three rings (you don't) and starts juggling continuously, sending the rings a little higher than normal and counting out loud. You watch closely, concentrating very hard and following the flight of the rings.

Your partner must continue juggling, no matter what (a lot of strange things can happen here), until you **take** all three rings.

◆ As your partner does a three ring continuous cascade, focus on the one ring as it comes **out of** your partner's right hand. Reach immediately **up and in** with your **Start Hand** (R hand in our illustration) and grab the ring at the **top of its** arc. It will help for your partner to keep counting out loud (1, 2, 3... 1, 2, 3...) until you take them all.

◆ After you grab the first ring, **immediatel** reach **across and up** to the other side wit your left hand and grab the ring no peaking out of your partner's left hand.

52

♦ As you stand with one ring in each hand, your partner has continued and let the third ring go up. **You take over now** and as the third one peaks, you get ready to use it to start into your continuous cascade.

♦ Then it's your partner's turn to repeat the above steps and **take back** the three rings from you. **"Takes"** is the key word- you keep juggling until they are all gone- no matter what (a.k.a "air juggling" or juggling the "space").

♦ **Continuous exchanging** - Once you are able to take the rings back and forth on an occasional basis, try doing it "every time" so the rings are exchanged with *each* cascade. One person does a one cascade pass (during which the rings are taken by your partner- so you don't catch any). Then you **immediately** take them back, and repeat. So you end up juggling like one person- you throw, she catches; she throws, you catch- it's a rapid exchange... and it's a blast!

Passing (a.k.a. The Six-Ring Circus)

This takes a little work - but it's so much fun, it's worth it! You will need six rings for this grea
and we've got 'em (see ordering information p. 63).

READY
AND...

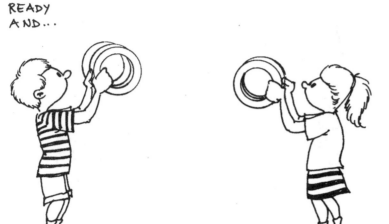

♦ Both partners have three rings held
same way and at eye level (two in
right hand and one in the left), and
ready to juggle. Stand opposite each ot
about seven feet apart with your hands
at eye level.

One person says "ready *and* go".

On "go", you both smoothly **drop-yo
hands-down** to the **Basic Start** posit
and immediately **begin cascade juggli**

GO!

♦ Look **through** your pattern to "see"
your partner's pattern while noticing
(but not watching closely), your own.
You can practice this by watching
yourself (not the rings) in a mirror
while juggling (see p. 37).

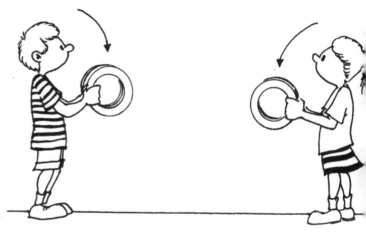

ONE &
TWO &
THREE &

♦ **Get in sync.** It is important that both s
of rings are being juggled at **roughly**
same speed and height. You want to h
the **same tempo.**

ONE &
TWO &
THREE &

Do a pre-passing exercise by juggling your three while counting "**1 and 2 and 3 and throw**", "**and 1 and 2 and 3 and throw**" (don't actually throw the ring yet). You say a number **each** time you send from your **R** hand and an "**and**" each time from your **L**.

Repeat this cycle three times, stopping after you say "throw" each time.

Check your timing so that each person's last ring lands **at the same time.**

ow!

♦ Go for it! Face each other seven feet apart, and begin your cascade as you did initially (Step 1). Count "**1 and 2 and 3 and**", throwing it straight across on the "**and**" after 3.

Concentrate on **sending it accurately up and over,** straight across to your partner's **left** hand from your right. Always look at your target (their hand) first and then after you toss your ring there, look for their ring coming towards you (surprise!).

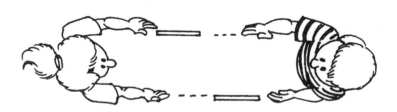

Slow down! Make your throws across a little higher and lazier. Do this a number of times. In other words, continue "1 and 2 and 3 and throw" until it feels comfortable.

♦ **Now keep going.** Catch with your left hand and **continue juggling,** counting "1 and 2 and 3 and". Remember to say "1" as you **receive** the incoming ring in your left hand from your partner.

Do this pass (i.e. sending a ring across) three times, then stop. Pause, breath deeply smile, and reach for your favorite beverage to toast each other!

Psssst. Want to know the BIG secret? It's found in the numbers "3-3-10".

When you see pro jugglers do this routine with clubs, hats, knives and other items of extreme craziness, their secret is 3-3-10. The way it works is that each **third** ring (thrown on "3 **and**") goes over to your partner **three times.** Then you switch so that every **second** ring i.e. "1 and 2 and" is sent across from your right to his left (also three times). Then **every** ring that lands in your right hand is passed across ten times and then you stop. It looks like this:

"Ready and go"

1 and 2 and 3 "and send" ↗ 3X
1 and 2 "and send" ↗ 3X
1 " and send" ↗ 10X

On this last round count - "1 and 2 and 3 and 4" etc. (up to 10), sending a ring each **time** you say an "and".

Dr Bob's Ultimate Variation (This oughta get you!)

Bounce to your partner

♦ Using the same routine as we just learned for the six ring circus and the bouncing technique described on page 15. Go for it... carefully.

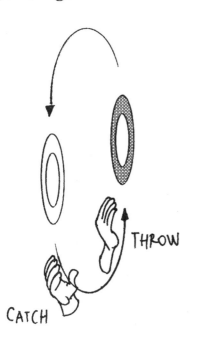

- First of all, you need to work on **one hand at a time,** independently. Juggle two rings three times with one hand. Then do it with the other hand. Toss the rings from inside to outside (see Fountain of Rings p. 36)

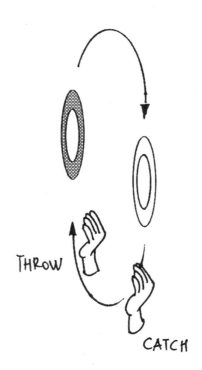

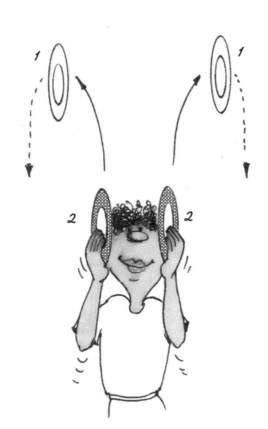

- **Two From Each Hand - at the same time:** Hold two rings in each hand. Send one ring simultaneously from each hand. As those rings peak, send the next two and catch the first two. Keep this identical rhythm pattern going without stopping. Do three passes.

♦ **Alternating - Two from each hand at different times:** This creates the illusion that the rings are crossing and that you're "**cascading**" four. They're not, and you're not. Each hand still works separately, only now on **different** rhythms. Counting does help here.

Start by saying "**1**" and send a ring, then immediately say "**2**" and send a ring quickly from the other hand. Then with **no pause**, say "**3**" and send again from the first hand; and finally say "**4**", and send the last ring. Just do this cycle once, catch all the rings (sure buddy!) and stop. Repeat the cycle three times. The rings do not stray across the mid-line of your body. They are caught by the same hand they were sent from.

Then try it twice in succession: **1, 2, 3, 4 - 1, 2, 3, 4**; and stop. Then go for continuous.

If possible, use two rings of the **same colour in one hand** and two of another colour in the opposite hand so you can pick up "strays" as they sneak over into the other hand (a "no no" in this trick).

Once you get two rounds in succession, then go for more rounds to help you get quicker and smoother with this.

Now check out **www.instantjuggling.com** for other **four ring tricks** (like columns or the hi-lo cascade) plus more tricks, neat juggling product stuff, tips and questions answered!

♦ Hold three rings in your **Start Hand** and none in the other hand.

♦ Throw them rapidly up (higher) and over to the other hand. **Count as you did for passing - "1", and** (send); **"2", and** (send); **"3", and** (send). Ring **"3"** is on its way as you catch **1**.

Now let's increase your speed and **confidence**, still with three -- **Be Patient!** Rapidly throwing ring 1, 2 and 3 in quick succession. Catch **"1"** and **toss it back** (before **"2"** arrives); catch **"2"** and toss it back; catch **"3"** and toss it back. It looks like this:

Send right (hand)... R
Send R...
Send R...
Catch & toss left (hand)... L
Catch & toss L...
Catch & toss L...

Do this step twice, stopping only when all three are back in your **Start Hand**. Then don't stop. **Continuously** send all three rings back and forth from your right and left hands as long as you can.

- Now you're a true speed demon and ready for five! Hold three rings in your **Start Hand** and two in the other.

- Send from **R** - (ring **1**)
  Send from **R** - (ring **2**)
  Send from **R** - (ring **3**)
  ...in rapid succession.

- As ring **1 peaks** and starts to come down, quickly send first and then second rings "**4**" and then "**5**" from left hand.

- Catch "**1**" in your left hand; then "**4**" in your right and keep alternating until you complete one cycle.

- Stop after one pass... and then repeat this pass again...

- Then go for **semi-continuous juggling.**
  Do two complete cycles/passes first and then try three cycles.

- Then, show your true obsessiveness and go for unlimited, **continuous five ring juggling,** stopping only for sustenance or relief, because your ring therapist shows up for your daily treatment!

If you **really** insist on doing this, I refer you on to Dave Finnigan's excellent book-"The Complete Juggler", and then to the Mayo Clinic for assessment and counseling! You're gonna need it!

P.S. The world record is **Eleven.**
Any takers?

Good Luck!

Dr. Bob's Final Words of Wisdom...

Well... hmmm.... Gosh! Believe it or not... I'm outta words! Now it's your turn, just like my friend John-

"Many years ago, as a kid, I tried to teach myself juggling and gave up. In thirty minutes with Dr. Bob's Instant Ring Juggling Book, I was amazing myself with my skills and wanting to show off in front of my wife."

John McIntyre (age, vintage)

So give me a ring sometime or drop me a line by fax, email, snail mail or carrier pigeon, because we love to hear from you. You can also visit our site on the world wide web at: **www.instantjuggling.com**.

We have **prizes** for the three best, most humorous ring juggling stories, and the three most original new tricks. Here is a picture of our judges (they're just animals) warming up for their job.

Au revoir ring masters!

Your friend,

Dr. Bob

The Products, Workshops, Prizes and Website Page

Products: Dr. Bob's Airborne Catalogue of Interesting Juggling Stuff (it's free)

For more juggling rings, balls, cubes, books, T shirts and other great juggling stuff- write, call, email or visit our website for your free copy of Doctor Bob's Instant Airborne Catalogue:

> Woodburn Life Balance Associates
> 328 Woolwich Street
> Guelph, Ontario N1H 3W5
> Phone (519) 763-4995: Fax: (519) 763-7957
> Email: bob@instantjuggling.com
> Website: www.instantjuggling.com

Workshops and Supersessions: Dr. Bob frequently travels all over the world to deliver motivational sessions (see author's notes p. 64)

- ♦ **Workshops:** How to lighten up, balance and juggle all the important parts of your life; so you get extraordinary results and have a ball doing it.
- ♦ **Supersessions:** an exciting and fun exercise in mass juggling and enjoyment. Dr. Bob has taught groups as large as 5,000 people to juggle, while giving them a new slant on taking care of business, being balanced and keeping all the balls in the air.
- ♦ **The Coaching Conversation:** Dr. Bob will coach small executive teams on the "juggling tool set" designed to stimulate your people to extraordinary performance and results.

Prizes and Contests: Check out our special Instant Ring Juggling prizes and mailing list.

- ♦ Outstanding prizes for your funniest, most adventuresome ring juggling **anecdote** or **original new trick.** Send by word, picture, movie, video or animation to our address.
- ♦ You can register your story or trick idea on our **electronic mailing list.** We'll also inform you of cool juggling happenings and neat stuff in the juggling world.

Internet:
- ♦ Online catalogue/ordering
- ♦ Workshop & supersessions info/booking
- ♦ Dr. Bob's Online Tricky Tips

www.instantjuggling.com

About The Author

Best selling author (**The Instant Juggling Book**), consultant, speaker and president of two companies, Dr. Bob Woodburn is an acknowledged expert on life balance and how people learn best. He uses juggling as a rich tool to speak with audiences all over the world about **change, balance and lightening up** to gain extraordinary results for themselves and their organizations.

He has great passion for teaching people how to successfully take on challenges they may not believe they can handle, **and always have fun doing it!** He recently taught 5000 University freshmen to juggle (all at once) on their first day on campus.*

And he practices what he preaches! From congas (yep, he's in a rock band) to canoes, he is the eternal "player" who claims he's never come across a toy or a playful person he didn't like.

He lives in Guelph, Ontario and frolics wherever he happens to be!

And the last word goes to the Pattison family...

" I'm already juggling three kids, a job and a zillion other things, but still figured I'd never be able to keep any three 'normal' objects airborne. But Dr. Bob's book proved me wrong and I love it!"

Lynn (age 39)

"Now if I can just learn to do this while playing my Banjo, I'm in!"

Ian (age 42)

"Aw, it was easy!"

Kaitlin (age 10)

"We all had so much fun, I thought we were going to laugh our heads off!"

Emily (age 13)

"I love the bounces and it's too cool that my parents can juggle."

Sam (age 8)

"Yawn. Big deal. I've been juggling catnip rings for years!"

Diva the Cat (age 21, in cat years)

* **For information about Dr. Bob's workshops and presentations see p. 63.**